The Turpentine Tree

for Finn, Conor, August, Mia and Maris

The Turpentine Tree

Lynne Hjelmgaard

Seren is the book imprint of
Poetry Wales Press Ltd.
Suite 6, 4 Derwen Road, Bridgend, Wales, CF31 1LH
www.serenbooks.com
facebook.com/SerenBooks
twitter@SerenBooks

The right of Lynne Hjelmgaard to be identified as
the author of this work has been asserted in accordance
with the Copyright, Designs and Patents Act, 1988.

© Lynne Hjelmgaard, 2023
ISBN: 9781781727140
Ebook: 9781781727157

The publisher acknowledges the financial assistance of the Books Council of Wales.

Cover artwork: by Richard Adams: 'The Turpentine Tree', oil on canvas.

Contents

III A Standing Ground

IV The Turpentine Tree

'but the knowing and the rain
the dream and the morning
the wind the pain
the love the burning'

W.S. Merwin, *A Step At A Time*

I

Something Of You,
Something Of Me

That Summer In Maine

There was the dramatic ferry voyage over
to the island, the shelter of my father's shoulder
against a brisk wind and sea; the enjoyable way

he bit into his apple, an extra large bite.
Never seen anyone's head touch a ceiling
until the young doctor arrived.

Lying in bed with fever I was apprehensive
but curious. His tall, kind presence filled the room.
Don't step on anthills! I was running away

from a goat who was sniffing in the woods.
Ants were crawling up my legs. It was a dream
standing still, invading ants consumed me,

the goats my enemy. I was the centre of the world's
discomforts. My sister came to the rescue, not without
laughter and tears. It all happened: my mother

caught in a thunderstorm, sunlight breaking
through the pines, the long shadows
in the cabin, waiting for her return.

Stuyvesant Town

Father mellowed
into sweetness
in old age. Gentleness
has such power.

Mother forms lonely
fragments
in memory.
I think of her mostly

with questions, sometimes
as a child,
seeing them
from some great distance,

but knowing
the care I needed
was there.
How to describe

this confusion,
at the same time
who were they?
How did I come

to belong
to them, as a child does?
Yet they opened
a way forward,

gone from me
a long time before
they were
gone from me.

And I left them also.

Little Landscapes of Silence

Certain pebbles are just the right shape
for skimming across water,

a universal past time,
like walking up and down the same streets

over and over again,
greeting the neighbours when you have to.

I used to walk with him on the lower East side,
try to keep up as we searched

for his grey Studebaker Packard.
Where'd I park the damn car?

I felt a presence on the edge of my bed,
early in the morning, just before they called.

I'd never heard the noise the moon makes,
does the moon make noise?

There was the push to get there in time,
slipping on ice after landing in D.C.

My father's body is lying on the table
in a dimly lit room

already out and about,
making its way in the universe.

Father Naked

Father naked. That first embarrassment
as a child, of seeing him in the shower,

not daring to look, confused and excited
but also afraid. I used to meet him

at the top of the subway stairs at 6pm –
wait for his ghost-like face to emerge

from the crowd, wait for his smile,
his hand, to hear my quiet voice

next to his forceful one. A voice
whose resonance could affect my mood,

whether curious, consoling, cursing,
or later, choking back tears when I left

home for good. Is this the same man
who posed for a photograph in Paris

with a rifle and a grin, his army jacket
still in our closet, war medals in the drawer.

He only hinted at D-Day horrors
in old age: the backpack was too heavy,

he never learned to swim. This man
who used to cut my toenails after bathtime,

who stormed out of the house in a rage, and I
would walk long city blocks just to find him?

What Saturday?

What Saturday couldn't contain a swing and all that it has to offer:
a buzz from the other children, a reeling motion pulling us up and away.

Holding onto cold rusty chains, pink grooves form on the inside
of my palms and sting. Legs in the air, swing legs in the air, take to the sky,

eat the sky – away from the lawns enclosed with chain link fences,
Do Not Walk On The Grass, the housing project, echoes of traffic on FDR Drive.

Some afternoons I'd escape to the park to climb the rocks, find colourful
leaves, press them into pages of my book in our tiny kitchen on the sixth floor.

When December's dark evenings descended, a yellow moon
kept monstrous buildings at bay. I'd walk the long way home

to by-pass certain children, run up the steps of the bleak stairwell
instead of waiting for the whining lift. There was a muted silence

on the crosstown bus. Warm, snug, crowded and smelling of damp,
a layer of moisture formed on its windows. No longer able to look outside,

I'd avoid eye contact, seek anonymity, conscious of strangers, their gaze.
I'd draw pictures of a future on glass someplace else – stick silhouettes

of a family, house, city, with a slight feeling that one day
I'd slip away from here, yet still might find myself closer to home.

Summer Camp

Pine Bush, New York 1961

All eyes upon her, we watch the girl being dragged outside
to Flag Raising at 7:30 am. Still in her underpants,

she has refused to get ready one too many times.
We stand in an open field among tall sunny grasses,

birdsong chitchat, black-eyed Susans and bees.
The flag is being hooked on and hauled up. Did we

cross our hearts, sing *My country tis of thee, sweet land of liberty?*
The camp counsellor looks straight ahead,

holds the girl with a firm grip as she struggles to break free.
This is the woman I am. This is the girl who has to learn.

Just as we learn to make our beds first thing
in the morning and jump into the cold lake

for Instructional Swim. Army blankets with scratchy sheets
beneath them must be folded with hospital corners.

Water is a dark brown pool – murky,
bottomless with bleeping frogs and unidentifiable fish.

I pray for a catastrophe like a flood or a drought
so we can all be sent home. Later, when a campfire is lit,

bats circle our cabin, the heavens run dark with cloud cover,
even more dark. Night in the woods is strangely comforting.

Fireflies sparkle in a light drizzle. I forget
what happened that morning, I forget about this girl.

Open And Closed Spaces
Summer Camp

We follow the trail up the mountain to Sam's Point after a campfire,
leaving at dusk, walking through the night, carrying our simple
needs. Climbing the rocks, open mountain air leads to togetherness.
Excitement picking berries. Sharing our canteens, buckets, sleeping bags.
A newly found friend. We trudge along together.

Seeking solace and finding it alone – sitting under a tree, walking beside
a stream, running water where we drink. A door to the earth stands
slightly ajar. Those much-needed solitary moments to separate
from the group. So young as to understand nothing. But to feel this sadness.
Sleeping with her creased photograph hidden under my pillow.
The one thing to hold onto which can't be shown or talked about.

From the New Jersey turnpike, the New York skyline is a haze
of familiarity, love and distance. Will she be there waiting for me?
On arrival, I search through bus windows for her face. Thick layers of heavy,
humid air. When I finally spot her I'm disappointed by her expression. She
belongs someplace else. Not here among the crowd of parents.

There's a silk scarf I want to buy her from the corner store
with large windows. Pressing my nose against the glass, longing
to step into brightness. Wanting it for her.

Night Journey: On the Greyhound Bus

I trusted the soft-spoken driver,
the sound of his foot on the pedal,
the humming of the engine.

Once we reached the highway,
cocooned by other passengers,
I was coaxed into dreamless sleep.

Further south, past midnight, we stretched
our legs at a gas station – suddenly aware
of the closeness of strangers - and that first

wave of hot humid air. I knew
in the morning we would reach
sunny Richmond and I would run

into the arms of my father. I still love
that Richmond moon, that southern heat,
the Howard Johnson motel

with its neutral-coloured curtains,
pull-out bed and starchy whites.
My first taste of a sun shower

standing in the pool's shallow end –
sunshine and rain as astonishing
as the sudden happiness of my family.

Something Of You, Something Of Me

(Black & white photo, circa 1940)

Are you waiting for someone?
>   Light shines on your face in a New York
>   City before-the-war way,

the woman you will become still ahead of you.
>   Uptown, you're sitting on the steps of Hunter College,
>   in a plain summer dress, bare legs crossed,

waves of black hair held back with clips,
>   prominent cheekbones. You seem to be facing the world head-on,
>   stubborn, poised and ready, looking towards the street,

not at the camera with a knowing
>   I-am-lovely look on your face. Hands clasped together,
>   happy as I want to envision you, dream you.

I long to step into the photo, know you –
>   your face and mine, both looking away from the camera.
>   Can a child embody a parent's shadow-side, still?

The last time I saw you in your hospital bed,
>   I was very young though already a mother.
>   Older now am I more able to forgive

our failings, what was unresolved between us,
>   misunderstood, before we ran out of time,
>   before I could think of you as whole?

Grandma Mary

Her short stout body. Her black
leather purse full of treasures:
lipstick, powder, Wrigley's chewing gum.

Her sweet powdery smell –
Hungarian Yiddish broken English,
calling to me – *Sheina-meidala.*

Her freckled forearms
always picking up my pieces,
putting me back together again

like a puzzle.
A seamstress whose dress hems
were somehow crooked.

Her black leather tie-up shoes.
Her bunions walking with such a history
and courage to the subway on 34th street.

From A Wardrobe

When I folded my father's much-worn Boston University
sweatshirt in the hospice shortly after he died,

I parted with it reluctantly, then hastily handed
it to my sister, wanting to forget.

I used to spray my mother's perfume on my skin and wear
her negligée when no one was home. I'd dance in its sheer

silk and role-play dreamily to Johnny Mathis songs –
slipping into a pretend world of love and loveliness.

When I first met my husband, he adopted my long
woollen turquoise scarf. He wore it constantly,

layering it around his neck as if it had always belonged
to him. When he died I kept his favourite Hawaiian

print shirt hidden in my closet. Surely I could keep
his scent and rogue spirit safe in a plastic bag. Always.

Through the years I've gone through my wardrobe and
weeded it out like grass. Gone: my Mexican wedding dress

trimmed with white lace and light blue ribbon, bought
for me by a friend whose name I can't remember.

Gone: a woolly Scandinavian sweater that itched and
smelled like sheep, bell bottom jeans I decorated with trees;

skin-tight, high-waisted jeans that held everything in;
an old tweed suit that seemed to shrink every few years.

Certain items come to mind like a vague memory
but also cut down deep: my first winter coat, the red shoes

I refused to wear, the matching spring dresses Grandma Mary
made for my sister and me. I had recently lost my front teeth.

II

What We Had Was Love

The View

when I by chance
held the hand mirror

at a certain angle
and glanced behind me

your loving gaze
caught me unaware

unexpectedly
looking right at me

from your photograph
on the shelf

the suddenness
more true than real

the shock of you
here and happening now

About her

for Hanne

there is too much to describe about her
  way too much   pressing along
familiar pathways   throughout my body

so much so I can almost touch them
  but then the feeling disappears   she disappears
but I know her   at least have told myself   I know her

we've been friends   lifelong friends for more years
  than the ages of our youngest children   born
a few months apart   now   middle-aged

how can I say   feel   think   sense in this very moment
  that I don't know her   or there is this constant nagging
wait   yes   that's not true   I do know her

just not who she is now
  this is also unreasonable   we imagine or
have some ideas of who we are

through our present   language   appearance
  our present   pain   pain that has worked its way in
or comes along   stays in the body   and never disappears

I think or believe when I say we know each other
  what I'm really saying is yes   we know each other's pain
we see it   I recently wrote

in my journal – oh
  I miss the woman with the fresh
blue glistening eyes   that woman   that face

Enter: The Bluest Bay

for Jan

Your studio always has that familiar smell
       of ageing plants, turpentine and paint.
Busts and figures placed near the bay window
       keep lookout, wary of the outside world.
Their features and curved willowy bodies
       are more affecting with the years,
as if reaching out to old friends
       to hold and protect. With tenderness,
always tenderness, your works fill the walls.

Enter: the bluest bay, the bow of a ship,
       Tordenskjold and the Danish Queen
wearing her trademark hat carved in low relief;
       a yellow house – in the background faint lines suggest
the remains of birch trees now gone a few hundred years.
       A strange woman with penetrating blue eyes
sadly stares into the beyond –
       tones of sepia and amber encircle her face
like a thin veil. A widow, a bride?
       Darkness on her one side, light enveloping the other –
your many selves displayed in shadows and silhouettes?

But you are truly the brown-eyed boy
       seated in a kayak holding court with seagulls,
feeding them, coaxing them, laughing
       as you row the oversized oars
that are longer than the days and nights you seek to capture.

What We Had Was Love

Orvieto, Italy

Bats were circling the bell tower,
their flapping wings rising and falling

above the cypress trees.
A streak of light blue sky

was comforting in the darkness,
as were ancient archways and walls,

a flickering candle, after dinner drinks
on the terrace. Everyone else had left,

including your partner.
We hardly knew each other

or stories about frescoes in the Abbey
and Etruscans who once lived here

in a labyrinth of caves.
But there was something more we knew

that we couldn't name. It was just there
as we spoke. Just there, until it wasn't.

When I saw you at breakfast in the morning
I wanted more than a few awkward goodbyes.

Evening Flight from Copenhagen

When I look out the window   the universe seems more
        confrontational   a last ray of sunlight lingers   on an edge of cloud
            as the plane dips to turn

white caps merge   on the Kattegat
        under the long bridge   almost Lego-like
            to Sweden   Godzilla   could break it in half

But there are other distractions   an ugly power plant   a dirty
        swimming pool enclosed by a hedge   parking lots
            dried-up fields   isolated country roads

The earth looks bejewelled joyous and unreachable
        because of course it is   from this height
            just as you are   unreachable   the younger you

who looked in my direction   but couldn't grasp the person I'd become
        in my dream   Did you feel unloved   were you angry
            did you remember my tendency   to unhinge

A man's watching a film on his I-pad in front of me
        It reflects back through my porthole   I enjoy it   so to speak
            from the outside of the plane   Godzilla-like

no language no meaning no matter   only flashing lights
        coloured images   ghosts flying away   uncomprehending
            bodies moving   back and forth in time

Honey

When my fingers slide over
a sticky spot on the kitchen counter
the memory returns –

of heating milk,
of groping for honey
in the dark.

A search for sweetness
and comfort
to quiet the night's disturbance –

travelling in a dream from one airport to another,
separation from my loved one.
Where were we going

that seemed so important at the time?
Now the dream is lost,
and so is the loved one –

thick and cloudy
honey in a jar
needs warmth and attention

before it once again
can become smooth, before it loosens
onto the spoon and runs free.

'You Are Cold – In Erotic Gaiety – Or Unhappiness'

The book I was reading called *Seduction and Betrayal* is now
at the bottom of the pile but I still finger through chapters,
hoping to better know Sylvia Plath, Dorothy Wordsworth,
the Bronte sisters– austere and difficult, mostly tragic lives.

Periodically I live with Akhmatova's life and poetry, 'Anna
of all the Russias', not only for her love poems but
also, to gaze at photographs of all her men. Was she happy
or unhappy? How she seemed to float above them. She admitted
that if she hadn't left one of her lovers, she would have forgotten
how to write poetry.

Men from my past sometimes appear in dreams, often
with affection – I once made love in the Paris Metro
with a younger man who carried my suitcase up endless
flights of stairs. But anger (theirs or mine) at some imagined
betrayal or misunderstanding. Or a coldness I hadn't noticed before,
uneasiness when separated at train stations or airports
or travelling in opposite directions; when they turn
their backs on me or walk by without looking in my direction.

In dreams, I run to catch a ferry alone when an old friend appears.
He buys each of us an ice cream cone, what they call 'soft ice'
in Danish. He said we both deserved them. But
they are whopping big, more than I can handle.

Mostly, I've been lucky, though I envy the innocence
of my twelve-year-old granddaughter who sings along
to the lyrics of Taylor Swift's love songs; the swinging
up and down notes, until another handsome face
waits across a crowded room.

I Thought I Revealed Nothing

You spoke to me, not with words
though you were so good with words.

I immediately trusted your voice
because of the light surrounding it,

its intonation and cadence.
There were other voices,

people moving around us –
it wasn't just what you didn't say –

you looked up
after signing your book

to see underneath, to what lies hidden,
what I foolishly tried to hide.

In Paris

Such certainty is beautiful,
but uncertainty is more beautiful still.
                    Wislawa Szymborska

We wandered together within our own square mile.
        Did we need the Louvre or Jardin du Luxembourg

after sharing a *salade niçoise* and half a carafe,
        your slippers placed beside the bed?

You much older, clearheaded, true,
        wished you could be younger for me

and I uncertain, afraid of losing again.
        We talked about an imagined future,

a trip around the world
        knowing we never would do it, the rest

of the day spent in our room
        holding each other, holding the afternoon.

For Dannie

This morning on the path
two magpies linger
until the very last moment.

For a few seconds I'm afraid
of losing my balance, of my feet
stepping on their tails or wings.

Do they sense
deep in their magpie bones
they will mate for life?

In the woods a young couple
walk towards a clearing in an open field.

Do they know the touch of a loved one
can reach his beloved
when he is no longer there?

Do they know happiness
has to be given back?

In the Walled Garden

In the walled garden, behind the magnolia trees
where we once sat and idled away the afternoon,

happiness rises in the air. Grief is its heavy shadow,
its cunning waits for an opening, a chance,

until it arrives subtly with the smell of freshly cut grass.
When I'm close to the exit of the park it fades, lets me slip away.

Once again I'm able to enjoy the goings-on and conundrums
sparrows make beneath a yew tree, and children just let out of school.

They run, question, fight, scream, full of laughter and demands,
so much themselves, they're in another country.

During the night, life itself quiets down,
is not kept awake by noisy death.

Absence

They deepen the world –
         lifelong friends

or friends who haven't been
         together for some time.

When we finally meet
         we can still laugh

at a familiar story
         or gesture

and between us know
         what's being thought, not said.

Do we seek
         our younger selves

inside each other,
         the person no longer here?

Many have left us now
         but absence rearranges itself

like water, like light.

Sometimes I forget how much

Sometimes I forget how much
I have loved certain men.

They are still close,
yet light years away.

I have written to them in the dark,
asked them questions

with my right hand,
hoping through the tears and anger

they will answer me with my left.
The truth has everything it needs.

It swirls around me
again and again,

not the person I was yesterday
but someone else,

here and now, who always wants –
wants more.

When Dawn

and every living thing
is the age it's always been
and continues – bird, tree, bush, you
standing on your two legs again.

You get to see me alive
I get to see you not dead
strange but familiar.
There is no information

only dreams of what came before
or may come after
and all that we may not want to know
when dawn comes running.

Look at him

Look at him walking briskly back from the dead

       Doesn't look you in the eye or leave a shadow as he passes

Not a hair or shirt collar out of place, even the crease in his trousers is neatly pressed

       No room for error or disappointment, for the sloppiness of life

He continues up the mountain without losing his stride

       There's only the climb, the climb

Bandits

Back then we were like bandits
escaping Babylon before its collapse,
our only prize: each other.

Lying together for the first time
overjoyed, half-afraid,
will you be mine

safe under the blanket
of your breathing?
When we left

the States for Denmark
we packed everything
including the pots which also,

on arrival, deepened
your mother's surprise. You,
my middle-of-the-night

golden ghost, slice of
yellow moon peeking
through the blind.

Ghost Patterns

At a certain hour someone walks
from room to room, the curtains are open

and the lights are out. Perhaps the moon is there,
if not there is the darkness to want and to touch.

Night reveals its vast field of the temporary –
the song of longing is the song of you.

The air has changed, the impressions, the house, the dark, love, you
who always forgive and are forgiven.

The drumming the pounding the singing the song.

They Move Further and Further Away

Loss solidifies for each year that passes
and at the same time we lose our grip

hundred-fold in cumulative time,
still wonder *Where are you?*

And yet they visit us everywhere –
share the same table, bed, walks,

accompany us into the world.
A stranger's face, his eyes,

kindness behind them,
the sly smile could be your kindness

as I imagine you now – could be your mind.
I look at a piece of dried bark

and grasp its longing to feel.
I'm content reading out loud

in early evenings – uninhibited,
speaking before an audience

of lizards and trees.
My body demands this nourishment,

all that I want.
My father's wrinkled face

among strangers at Miami Airport,
still there.

Deluge

A sprinkling turns to downpour,
the ailing world enters
my window.
May it wash our ills away –
says my whispering voice
– this is where I live,
but do I *live* here?

Should we stay inside, stay away,
is safe right, right where I am,
can I take it – can my children,
will their children's children,
will they fix things, can anyone,
does the world?

Almost summer.
The sycamore more floral,
deep and full of intensity,
next to the purple burgundy leaves
of its neighbour –
yet unidentified –
all my loves near to me.

III

A Standing Ground

Your Journals Have

Your journals have become more precious with age,
      their contents still undefinable,
            covered in blemishes, psychedelic

ink drawings, sporadic stains of ancient glue.
      But they seem to gather wisdom
            by their plain existence,

and are magnified with importance,
      even with torn bindings
            and fragile loose pages.

I sometimes read between the lines
      to form entire thoughts
            from your scribbled Danish,

the handwriting changes according to mood
      and energy, brain waves of a self
            that alters from day-to-day.

It's thrilling to happen upon
      a clear complete sentence,
            but if I don't leave a marker

it disappears into an abyss.
      Oh to know what happened when
            you were constantly on the move,

diaries weathered with dirt, cigarette butts and sweat.
      Oh to find that secret place
            within you, a key to turn, to be let inside,

become more aware – of what? And why?
      Our history has changed. In one journal though
            I find the light green crumpled paper

of your horoscope dated 1970, Ville Park (East) Bombay.
      I still squint to read it at 70 as I did at 20,
            trying to confirm my entry

and significance in the section on marriage,
            wife, family and children.
                        But then a page in the journal falls open

to a surprising declaration:'I have just counted mosquito bites
        on my right arm, 43 there were! From the top
                of my right shoulder to my fingertips.'

1969

After the march on Washington we decided to drive to Florida
        or tried to. What did we eat besides pancakes and weed?
There were six of us, we could only pay for one motel room.
        I remember lying next to Dave – the floor was good –
wanting to get closer to him but he had a girlfriend who wasn't there
        and he was loyal. Sydney loved me,
though I didn't love him back but liked him well enough
        to be semi-attached because of Paul. There was also Vic
with bleached blond hair who left me for Emily, a natural blonde.

We ran out of money and decided to turn around, reluctant to drive
        through the deep South where there was a hatred
for men with long hair. A few months later
        after an early morning raid in the dorms,
Sydney and Vic had their heads shaved in the South Jersey county jail.
        The police thought me innocent and let me go.

The Copenhagen Hair Salon
for Berith

When she was old enough to slowpoke around me
in her small red Danish clogs, we'd play beauty parlour.
I was her willing subject and happily sat on the floor.

She'd fuss over my long dark hair, throw a hand mirror
and magazines onto my lap so I could follow
her inventions and entertain myself

as she brushed my hair to remove tangles, rearranged it
in elegant styles; piling it on top of my head or
roughly, not intentionally, pulling it away from my face.

She'd talk with other imaginary customers in the room
in her newly-formed language; at times in a whispering voice
I found so comforting – I'd fight to stay awake.

This dreamy state of beauty and curls I could instantly partake in.
In Danish, her two year old vocabulary sounded so sensible.
Her mutterings and sighs contained an abundance of power

drawing me in - in to all the places I've never been
and always wanted to go;
her will stronger – more mine than mine.

Bird Seconds

Close, but not too close – just
        an ordinary hopping-out-of-a-bush-blackbird

immediately in front of me.
        He's fast as inbreath, we spy each other,

will this fear ever stop?
        Wanting, finding, breaking away –

in bird seconds his beak holds a berry,
        I wait for delightful singsong that never arrives.

I'm usually timid around birds.
        As a child I was afraid of their innate power,

their flapping wings if hovering too close.
        I sensed otherworldly spirits

that could prey on weakness,
        giving them qualities I couldn't even name.

Creatures with pointy beaks that could nibble your fingers.
        I was told their blood was purple.

Guilt still remains at having tortured my sister's parakeet
        with an ice cream stick.

I wanted to make Squeaky squeak.
        What did his vision behold

besides a sweaty human peering into the cage,
        wanting revenge, wanting to dominate,

also yearning for release – to rise
        and roam above.

Grandkids

for Finn, Conor, August, Mia and Maris

Running through parks,
      running till the perfect stick is found
            to be used in battle,

to protect the territory,
      to ford a stream, for playing house
            or job, playing wounded,

playing dead. One day
      they will think of me as dead,
            forget mostly (as I sometimes do

my lost loved ones) what I feel like,
      smell like, sound like.
            They come to me all smiles

wearing a t-shirt backwards –
      arms, legs longer than yesterday,
            their open faces waiting for my embrace.

Now we speak occasionally to say hi.
      I regard them from a distance
            and watch as hours pass

behind closed doors where they tend to marinate
      and emerge with a chin more rounded
            or a sharpened profile.

What She Gave Me

a locket meant for a chain
I never wear
a little amber angel with pointed wings
and big feet

couldn't prevent
how weary the air became
between us
it lies faithfully

in my carved wooden box
next to the Bahamian sand dollar, still intact
and Hindu prayer book on love
and friendship

how brief our connection was
how delicate
the inner threads
holding up its wings

Your Late, Late New Year's Card

for Laure

I don't expect it before end of January
or even February. 'How did we get here?',

you wrote this time from Paris.
Knowing each other since before

the Eiffel Tower started to sparkle at dusk.
Knowing each other since before Tess,

now in her twenties, was born and you
phoned to say, 'I had her'. When we

confided, gossiped and cried
in your small flat on Rue Violet and Franck

would disappear into the kitchen to cook.
How many walks did we walk all over Paris,

my suitcase trailing behind me?

Blaen Ddol

I was a good distance from the bend in the road
      when I first heard her: a woman posing for a photograph

in front of the whole herd, their heads lined up together.
      She was perched on a grassy mound just beneath the fence, all laughter.

Deep down from-the-belly, unstoppable laughter.
      For those moments it seems the cattle let her enter their domain.

They peered at her closely, as if recognizing a friend,
      one who had just stroked or fed them, made them feel secure.

Now she belonged to them. Just yesterday, a lone white cow
      with dark brown markings moved away when I tried to approach.

Perhaps she was feeling as thin-skinned as me, alone on this country road,
      away from all that is familiar, intimate, and dear.

Am I as strange to her as I am to myself
      when I allow outsiders and the world to vex me?

An accidental planting swaying back and forth
      in the wind until some roots take hold?

A Love Affair Between A Border Collie And A Wire-haired Sausage Pup On A Small Building Site

She brings him bits of an already chewed-upon
plastic bucket or what looks like
a petrified twig. He can't wait to greet her,
doing a kind of Don Juan leap and jump.
When most feverish, this hairy little bearded body
covered in wood chips and dust
searches the grounds for whatever she can find
to please him. He receives the smallest of treasures
with great delight. Sometimes, so involved with
her digging, she forgets him, though any bark,
whimper, or sideways glance in his direction
is not lost. He waits loyally, patiently.
The truest connection. Anything can happen
with such affection in the air.

Two Photos
for Kim

Take the photo of a young boy
in a Philadelphia sweatshirt,
baseball banners hung on the wall
behind him. He's an innocent,
cheerful thirteen, fringe smoothed flat

on his forehead. We always seemed
to be in sync, my lap often occupied
until the day he outgrew it. I look at
the photo and try to place myself.
How little I knew. How much I wanted.

In a more recent photo the grown man
doesn't face the camera. His hair
is windblown, sunglasses cover his eyes,
hands are loosely placed on the wheel
of a boat, face tilted in silhouette.

There were the countless times
he had stood on deck
when his father was still alive –
coiling lines, unpacking sails.
Waiting, listening. Devoted.

Knowing what needed to be done
with unspoken ease
and closeness –
the thin wire tightrope of love.
You know it's there
though sometimes you can't walk it.

A Standing Ground

These are adult children.
I've taken them so far –

don't know anything different
than this hard love and

the darkness it sometimes brings
as the train pulls out of the station,

rolls through the English countryside.
Uprooted, I long for them,

a home – but if not for them
where would a home be?

What would I choose – a path
through the woods

where tree roots branch
and weave,

the same woods from
childhood summers?

There You Were

A sadness worked its way to stomach, chest,
choking throat. I was waiting in line for shrimp
and fries, hoarding packets of ketchup and mayo

because they're free in San Francisco.
I forgot about my dizziness walking
vertical avenues to the harbour.

I forgot about the fisherman in flimsy flipflops,
thin worn trousers, a meagre fishing line
perched on his back. A fat seagull posed

at the edge of the dock for a selfie,
he knew all about throat-chest-belly cries.
Full of himself and fish, and I diminished

next to him unable to speak or eat,
my teeth tearing into a wet ketchup packet
trying to hide my outburst from our son,

so much like you now – in manner, looks and
strength, you. He sat calmly at a corner table,
overlooking the bay, this grown man in his prime.

The Photograph Answers

for Stig

I love to speak of you to those who will listen
      or to the few who knew you intimately –
            your children, of course.

I stare at a blank wall and order it to bring back
      certain moments – even the years
            I still searched for you in a crowd.

Did *we* really exist? Yes –
      the photograph answers. A warm
            summer evening, sunlight

crowning the top of our heads, the moon
      a dim shadow. We sat together, deeply engaged,
            sharing the same thought.

Annalise

Sometimes I visualize Copenhagen and see your death
in the middle of winter. Bone chilling grey. Sharply cutting.
Packed ice. During the service while squeezing the hand of
your son I was so overwhelmed by your coffin disappearing,
came the tears, came floods of tears. It has been years now
since your ashes were laid in *De unkendets grav.* Humbly.
Not to leave a mark. That was you.

It never fails. As soon as I land in the airport my legs begin
to wobble. I board an SAS bus and people like aliens speak
a tongue I no longer have a tolerance for. Long throaty vowel
soundings, hardened guttural pronunciations grasp my throat,
reach a hand way down inside my chest. As we proceed down
the motorway, row houses appear with soft glowing lamps in
windows lit like buoys at sea. I follow them with my eyes
hoping it will give me a glimpse of you or your house named
Karma. Degnemose Alle – its subtle shades of colour in winter,
fragrance of the lake in summer.

We no longer walk together with the children down the dirt
path running alongside your garden or feed the ducks stale
bread under the willow tree where the swans always laid,
protecting their fuzzy-headed new-borns in spring. Much
of Denmark's blossoming left with you.

During your last visit to the States I had the audacity
to get annoyed. There you stood carved up on your left side
with one lung removed. It was something about helping
yourself to the last yoghurt in the refrigerator. Of course
you should and I tried to stress this! I relive that moment
many times. Your hurt expression brought all of my questions
to a head. And you waving goodbye at the airport
knowing it might be the last time.

April

Now that the cherry tree
has blossomed

a gale-like wind
comes along

and blows
its petals away.

Thankfully, some remain.
I listen to the howls,

to every gust,
then assess the damage,

gather my forces
together again.

Last night you paid me
another visit.

It had been too long
you said,

there was nothing more to say.
This morning the tulips

seem to jump out of
your mother's vase,

there isn't enough room for them
in the water.

IV

The Turpentine Tree

I'd Like To Speak Of This Memory

of hummingbirds, long ago fragrances
coconut and fig, fluttering wings next to
a hot, hot wooden deck underfoot

and trade winds blowing up the night
throwing our ship about
taut lines stretched to the limit and released

thrill of the wind working its way
through every inch of the rigging, no mercy
but to take over and blow, take over and blow

Fragments, The Sea

Humbled before its timeless drudgery,
we were forced us to get to the bottom of ourselves.

Even when I questioned
my endurance and loneliness,

sleep overwhelmed,
restlessness was relieved.

The nourishment of the sea
on our faces was a smell we understood.

The constant changing, the never imagined
heights it grew to,

a lifetime of gifts
contained in a few hours.

Departing Reedsville, VA.

from the Ship's Log

1

Frank, an old sailor from Wisconsin
was on his way to Florida
and liked it here so much he stayed.

He gave us a tour of the town and a history lesson.
George Washington was born 25 miles from here,
and Lee surrendered to Grant 30 miles away.
According to Frank, John Smith and Pocahontas lived here too.

The main thing we learned about Reedsville
was that it smelled like fish oil from a factory.
In a big way.

We couldn't wait to leave and
were happy to find Windmill Point.

2

Boy did we have fog on this leg.
The start was fresh winds beating close over the shoals.
A few hours of shortening sail was followed by no wind,
followed again by a breeze. Passing fish traps 65 degrees to port.
Course 140. Changing course to 145 due to set winds from South.
Norfolk is a giant harbour, warships everywhere.

3

They were lined up, one after the other.
Ghost ships from WW II
on the periphery of the war story.

I thought of my father on one of the ships,
along with hundreds of others.

During the night the mind darkens too.
Voices come,
you even talk to them.

To those far away or left behind
or those waiting for you in a dream,
especially when you're alone on 'dog' watch,
the sea pushing you along until dawn.

When everyone's sleeping below
it's hard to stay awake.
Is a good cure for insomnia.
The whole works.

He liked it here so much,
he stayed.

4

September's List:

Storm cover for main hatch.

Rebuild helmsman seat.

Build life raft box.

Install manual and auto bilge pumps.

Install jacklines and pad-eyes for cockpit, galley.

Fill propane tanks.

*Grab-bag and list for jobs during emergency
include medical kit.*

On The Atlantic Coast Of Spain

The wild does not have words
Tomas Transtömer

Large families dine together on the beach
at midnight – from elder to younger.
In the dark a herd of sheep senses something other.
Suddenly frightened, they line up and huddle together.
The culprit, a black cat, has ventured in too close,
grown bored and turned around.
Cold wind pushes against us in the open sea, tries to knock us down.
The ocean wants to kill you.
How far back does grief go, what is lost, what can be found?
Is memory transferred between us without words –
years later, is the unsayable felt?

The Turpentine Tree I

British Virgin Islands

The back door still opens
onto the turpentine tree
– a coppery faux god
with wildly twisted branches
and coveted peeling bark.

For each year that passes
it slips further into the void
with a torn t-shirt hanging
from its limbs and the company
of a heron and billy goat
enjoying the intimacy
of our outdoor shower.

It slips further and further
with prickly pear cacti
and golden century plants
near the alluring pinkish beach
and dangerous reef
that scares day trippers away.

It lifts out of the stony ground
mindful of cacti needles
and yellow eyes of rats relishing
our abandoned house,
and it flies into the eye of the storm.

Heading East

In the shipping lanes of the Straits which even then,
    more than twenty years ago,

were a graveyard for Africa, we, in our ignorance,
    sailed happily for Spain – our children

peering up from the cabin at headlands,
    snow-capped mountains of Morocco,

asking how much longer… mostly content
    to return to a book or stare blankly

at the water, doze. Their questions echoed
    my loneliness, longing for certainty,

land: stalls of fresh fish and pungent smells
    of spices, early morning parakeets

gossiping in jacaranda trees, sprinkles of
    a shower giving way to hot sun.

Now I try to decipher your writing in the ship's log
    for words of reassurance – I'm left with sea miles,

celestial calculations, course headings for each hour,
    pencil marks on a chart, a statue of Columbus

pointing the way out to sea.
    Did our happiness rely on a shared restlessness,

a search for a haven, a rope ladder for look-out,
    an escape from an undertow within?

I remember the sound of a distant gong –
    a channel marker, the sudden avoidance

of a freighter laden with cargo
    swinging dangerously in a heavy swell.

In your company there was always safety –
        in pitch darkness the sea a dreaming mind,

a soothing voice, by day a mirror, a window,
        a keeper of worlds loved and lost

working their way to the surface
        in yearning and sorrow.

Whale

Its briny smell in the wild
seemed to contain every creature
that once lived and died
on the seabed,
their long mournful breaths.

I don't recall what it looked like
or how it came upon us,
a dark fin barely caught
in the corner of my eye, as though
it wasn't meant to be caught

as we galloped along
crests of an abating swell,
in warm turquoise-green water,
sails tweaked to pick up speed.
It moved with a quick and steady grace,

seemingly out from underneath us,
leaving behind a cold turbulent wake
without so much as grazing the hull,
disappearing in seconds
into its own unfathomable longing.

World Travellers

You scatter when the planks
    of the ship are lifted
        to expose your hideaway

in decaying, bad smelling
    waters of the bilge.
        Cockroach, do you suffer too?

Homeless, unlovable,
    on the run? You must have hitched a ride
        in Miami,

scrambled aboard with fresh fruit
    and tins, ridden with us
        across the Gulf Stream

through the Bermuda Triangle,
    laid your eggs
        in crevices

under the floorboards,
    as we tacked
        in tremendous swells

in the Saragossa Sea.
    Now that we are safe
        in harbour,

there are American guests
    on board. I try to distract them,
        hide my disgust

when you make an appearance,
    long antennae
        leading you sideways

along the bottom
    of the galley wall,
        aiming for tiny cracks

in the wood. Larger
in the tropics you're still
the master of escape,

a Houdini in helmet
and chains. Survivor
of bug bombs

you creep up
from the gates of hell
to the top of the mast –

such togetherness, herd mentality,
brute strength. Should I pity you more
instead of wanting

the musical crunch of your body
underfoot, more numbed
than dead or just dead?

A Sailor's Lament

Our affection for it was instant
and sure. A painting that suggests
more than speaks, with enough

room to think and wander in –
a horseshoe bay, a secluded
stretch of sand, beaches

we had walked together and
left behind. Beaches that visited us
during our most solitary nights.

★★★

The taste of salt
still fresh in our mouths,
clothes and hair,

we chose the picture
together at the old market
in Dartmouth.

Deep marine tones hint
at depths further out, sky-blue
dominates the shallows.

A lone figure walks
close to a few skiffs.
Is he lost or close to home?

I think the truth is both.
Low grey shadows hover
beside a rain cloud

about to burst.
It must be England,
but it could be anywhere.

The Turpentine Tree   2

Coconut rats and goats befriend you,
unruly cacti have been chopped down,
geckos scramble to secret rendezvous.

The roof of our house lies partially in ruin.
I hear voices of beloveds, crashing surf,
a sense of promise still resides within them,

a welcome home. After a restless night,
I sit in the backyard. Your coppery limbs
are shiny, your branches curled

and questioning. Exposed.
Across the sound a whole volcanic vista
confronts me, triangular and pointed.

Into The Valley Of The Trough

Don't have to inhale it
to recognize its smell,
the sacred Gore-Tex essence.
Breathable, adaptable, a chemical
designed to repel moisture

in the open air. Not true for us.
Cursing the button at the top
of a jacket that won't shut,
a cold trickle of seawater
dripping down our spines,

stretched-out elastic in the hood,
cord strings choking our necks,
the icy draft. This conjures
whitecaps in a bay, sleek
fiberglass racing sloops,

a row of bodies seated for balance
on the high side, the skipper
steering on the low,
disappearing into
the valley of the trough.

To what depths and heights
do we hunt for joyful
encounters with the wind
and will they endure?
What happens to

a fumbling finger or foot,
a hand reaching
for a slippery grab-hold,
or the earth in the path
of its own swinging boom?

Acknowledgements

My warm thanks and appreciation to editors Zoë Brigley and Rhian Edwards for publishing this book. I am also grateful to the staff at Seren.

Thank you to the editors of the following publications where some of these poems first appeared and/or are forthcoming: *Acumen, Artemis, London Grip, Poetry Wales, Quill & Parchment, Shearsman Magazine, Stand, The Poetry Worth Hearing Podcast* and *The Royal Society of Literature website - Write Across London.*

Thank you to Mimi Khalvati and Jane Duran who read through the manuscript at its various stages. I'm most grateful for their careful readings, insightful comments and advice. I'm grateful to Wendy French for her comments and faithful reading of the manuscript. Thank you also to Jane Duran's Wednesday night group for their feedback, expertise and friendship.

I would like to thank Amy Wack, Nora Hughes, Sue Greenhill, Barbara Karban, Laure Millet, Jan Petersen and Richard Adams for his inspirational painting of *The Turpentine Tree* on the cover.

And always with love and appreciation to my children Berith and Kim and grandchildren Finn, Conor, August, Mia and Maris.

Notes

I am grateful to the writers and artists whose work inspired some of the poems in this book.

p. 13, *Little Landscapes of Silence* – The title was taken from a profile in The New Yorker, about the artist-poet Peter Sacks. He describes the first landscape drawings he made with food pigment from cucumbers, zucchini, tomatoes, peppers. '*They became little landscapes of my own silence.*'

p. 17, *Open and Closed Spaces* – Title after Tomas Tranströmer.

p. 28, *What We Had Was Love* – title from *A Memory*, Umberto Saba

p. 31, '*You are cold – in erotic gaiety – or unhappiness*'
Marina Tsvetaeva to Anna Akhmatova, from Tsveaeva's poem 'Your Narrow, Foreign Shape'.

p. 55, *Blaen Ddhol* is the name of a road a few miles outside of Aberystwyth, Ceredigion, Wales.

p. 58, *A Standing Ground* – Title after Wendell Berry.

p. 61, *Annalise* – *De ukendets grav* is the *Graves for the Unknown* cemetery in Copenhagen.

p. 67, *Departing Reedsville, VA.* In italics: Stig Hjelmgaard's entry in the ship's log, on board *Annalise, September, 1984.*

p. 76, *A Sailor's Lament* is inspired by a painting by Lamoë.

p. 70,77, *The Turpentine Tree* was inspired by an actual tree in the British Virgin Islands on the island of Jost Van Dyke. It was in the back yard of a house destroyed in the hurricane of 2017.

By The Same Author

Distance Through The Water	(I Want Press 2002)
Manhatten Sonnets	(Redbeck Press 2003)
The Ring	(Shearsman Books 2011)
A Boat Called Annalise	(Seren Books 2016)
A Second Whisper	(Seren Books 2019)